CARVING WHALES AND DOLPHINS

Anthony Hillman

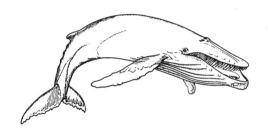

DOVER PUBLICATIONS, INC.
New York

Copyright

Copyright © 1996 by Anthony Hillman.
All rights reserved under Pan American and International Copyright Conventions.

Published in Canada by General Publishing Company, Ltd., 30 Lesmill Road, Don Mills, Toronto, Ontario.
Published in the United Kingdom by Constable and Company, Ltd., 3 The Lanchesters, 162–164 Fulham Palace Road, London W6 9ER.

Bibliographical Note

Carving Whales and Dolphins is a new work, first published by Dover Publications, Inc., in 1996.
These patterns and drawings are not to be used for printed reproduction without permission.

Library of Congress Cataloging-In-Publication Data

Hillman, Anthony.
    Carving whales and dolphins / Anthony Hillman.
        p.   cm.
    ISBN 0-486-29096-4 (pbk.)
    1. Wood-carving—Patterns.   2. Whales in art.   3. Dolphins in art.   I. Title.
TT199.7.H5475   1996
731'.832—dc20   95-52664
                                                                                                            CIP

Manufactured in the United States of America
Dover Publications, Inc., 31 East 2nd Street, Mineola, N.Y. 11501

How to Carve a Whale, Dolphin or Porpoise

In the last few decades more and more people have become interested in that group of marine mammals known as cetaceans, or the whales, dolphins and porpoises. Through aquarium exhibits, performing dolphin shows, studies by marine biologists and extensive media coverage, our awareness of these unique animals has been growing. People who don't live anywhere near the ocean have become familiar with the Gray Whale, Bottlenose Dolphin and of course the Killer Whale or Orca. It is common to see cutout or carved silhouettes of whales or dolphins fastened to homes near the seashore.

Yet, how well do we *really* know whales and dolphins? As I was doing the research for these patterns, I realized how distorted are our perceptions of, especially, whales, and how this distortion has affected our visual representations of them.

Whales are usually portrayed as immense, bloated, almost formless creatures with a tail at one end. In truth, even the largest living animal—the Blue Whale, measured at as much as 110 feet long—is actually almost serpentine in its proportions. We are just now beginning to appreciate whales and dolphins in the aesthetic sense, and I have tried to make these patterns reflect their true grace and beauty.

Whales can be divided most basically into two categories: those with teeth and those whose mouths instead have plates of baleen, or whalebone, a horny substance used to filter food out of the water. Dolphins and porpoises form their own groups within the larger group of the toothed whales. Porpoises are generally smaller than dolphins, lack the "beak" that is so conspicuously part of the head shape of many dolphins and are less likely to make acrobatic leaps out of the water.

This is a pattern book. It gets cut up as a matter of course. But before you cut it to pieces, *read the instructions!* Here are some general tips to keep in mind as you proceed.

WOOD SELECTION

For these carvings I used a soft wood for the bodies. Pine, white cedar or other suitable soft woods are fine. For the pectoral fins (more distinctively called flippers on whales and dolphins) and tail flukes, I used basswood (also called linden). This works well for relatively thin, fragile pieces because it has a fine, close grain and takes detail well. Explore what is available from sawmills in your area. Even a small amount of scrap construction lumber can yield enough wood to keep you busy for many winter nights.

I have indicated the dimensions of the wood stock necessary for each carving; these measurements are a little large, to facilitate sawing out the basic shape around the template (it is always easier when the blade of the saw can make one smoothly flowing, continuous cut).

EYES

Most people prefer glass eyes on wire for carvings to obtain a more realistic look. I have provided sizes in millimeters for each project (as for the color, all of these subjects have black eyes). Black glass eyes are available from most carving-supply houses.

Before you begin, read through the general instructions. Remove the staples from the book and spread the pages out flat. Decide which model you would like to carve. Read any specific instructions on the Plates describing special procedures for that carving. A #11 X-ACTO knife is excellent for cutting out the patterns. Go to it and have fun: that's what it's all about.

PREPARING THE BLANK FOR CARVING

You will notice I have provided profile, top and front views for all twelve species of cetaceans. The profile is the most important of these drawings. Please note that on the Long-finned Pilot Whale, Dall's Porpoise, Blue Whale and several other species I have included the dorsal fin as part of the profile to cut out *with* the body. This is usually because the dorsal is relatively small and thick and has an even thicker base as it joins the body. On the Blue and other whales with a very small dorsal fin, extra carving effort is necessary to give the proper thickness at the base of the fin.

The profile pattern also shows the location of the eyes and sometimes the blowhole(s). Also shown are the attaching points of the flippers and tail flukes. The profile pattern is the one to use as a template for sawing out the carving "blank," the name for the piece of wood that has been sawn out in the general shape of the carving but has not yet actually had any wood carved out it. Cut out the profile pattern carefully and place it on your wood stock. The grain should always run parallel with the top of the head. Trace the outline with an ordinary lead pencil (#2 or softer).

On the Dall's Porpoise and Narwhal the profile *includes* the tail. Be sure when sawing these patterns you don't cut the tail end too thin.

Once you have traced your pattern onto the wood saw out the profile. Next, measure the exact center of the thickness of the blank (from one side of the body to the other) and draw a centerline completely around the piece (see Fig. 1). Do not cut away this guideline, or you may ruin the pattern outline. The centerline should remain until final sanding; redraw it if it gets obscured during carving.

Before you begin to cut away any wood, it is impor-

tant to understand the final shape you want to arrive at. Study the patterns. You should supplement these with any reference material you can find, including drawings and photographs.

I caution you about using photos of stranded cetaceans; a whale's form becomes greatly distorted when it is not supported by water.

Fortunately, there are more and more books available with excellent photographs of live swimming whales, dolphins and porpoises.

The profile blank can be prepared further. Using the top-view pattern as a guide, mark off the corresponding top-view shape onto your cut-out profile. In most cases the top view will not be accurate if you actually try to trace this off onto the blank. A pair of dividers can be useful for transferring the necessary spacing from side to side (Fig. 2).

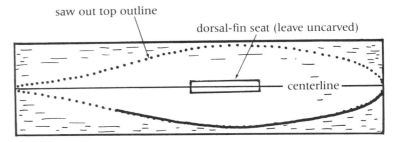

Fig. 2. Top View of Carving Blank

Once you have transferred an accurate set of reference marks from the top-view drawing onto your blank, saw out the top view, being careful not to take too much off around the head, as most saw blades leave tooth marks that must be carved out later.

On the above-mentioned patterns that include the tail, you must be very careful not to ruin this part of your carving. A jigsaw will usually be easier for cutting this out, providing there is enough clearance for the tail stock. (See the diagram "The Parts of a Whale.")

When sawing out the top view with those patterns that require the addition of tail flukes, it is important to saw the sides of the tail stock straight so that the base of each tail fin will fit flush with that surface. If you want to change the angle of the tail flukes you can use a small carver's plane to cant the surface of the tail stock.

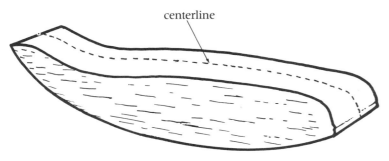

Fig. 1. Profile of Carving Blank

CARVING THE BODY AND HEAD

Study the three views I have provided for each project, as well as the photograph included on the cover. Some species' profiles do not show dorsal fins but instead have a strong "dorsal ridge." Examples of this are the Sperm Whale, the Gray Whale and espe-

(Instructions continue after Plates.)

Blue Whale.

The largest of all the whales, and one of the largest animals ever to have lived on earth.

Length to 110′

Dimensions of Wood Stock: 17″ long × 3¼″ wide × 3¼″ high

Flippers (2): 4″ long × 1″ wide × ¾″ thick

Flukes (2): 5″ long × 2″ wide × ¾″ thick

Eyes: 4mm

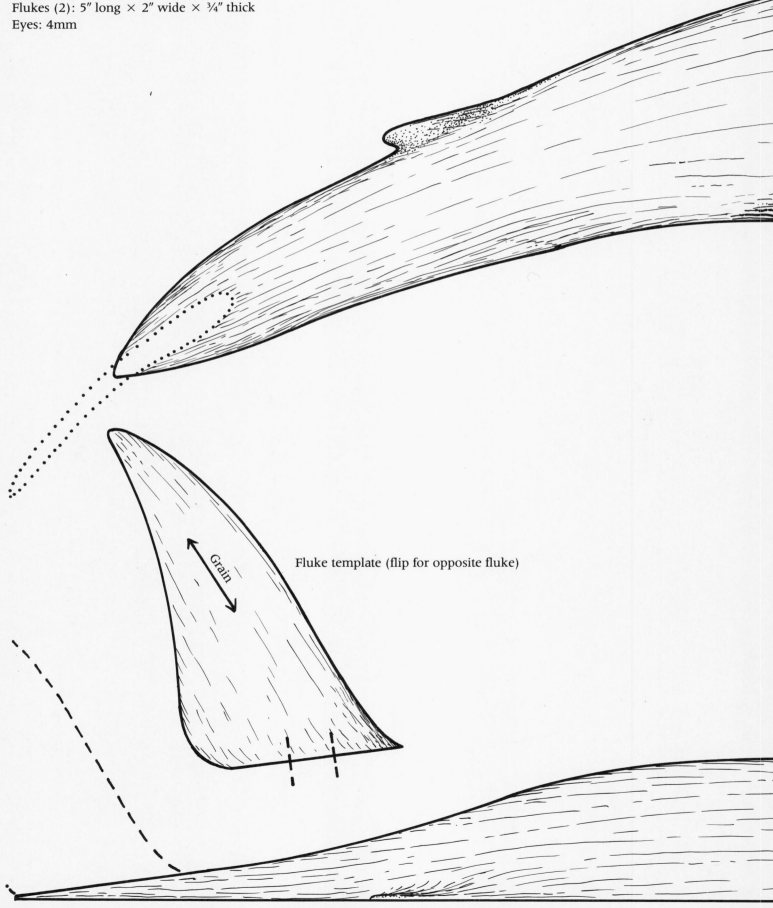

Grain

Fluke template (flip for opposite fluke)

Plate 1 *(left)*

Remove staples to see and use full patterns.

Dall's Porpoise.

A small porpoise with a robust body, this extremely fast swimmer is found only in the North Pacific Ocean.

Length to 7′
Dimensions of Wood Stock: 11½″ long × 3″ wide × 4″ high
Flippers (2): 2″ long × ¾″ wide × ½″ thick
(Dorsal fin and flukes cut out with profile.)
Eyes: 3mm

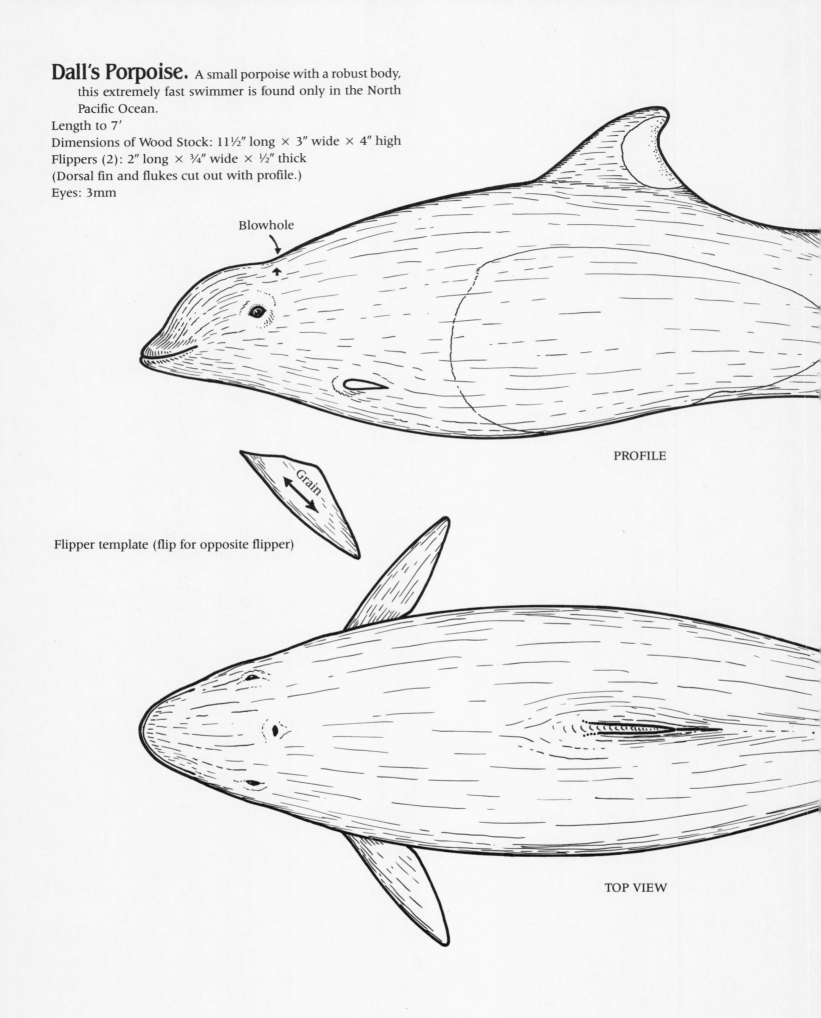

Blowhole

PROFILE

Flipper template (flip for opposite flipper)

Grain

TOP VIEW

Plate 2 *(left)*

Remove staples to see and use full patterns.

Common Dolphin.
This dolphin has the most complex coloration of all cetaceans—a striking pattern that is subject to considerable variation.

Length to 8′

Dimensions of Wood Stock: 10½″ long × 2″ wide × 2½″ high

Dorsal Fin: 2½″ long × 1¼″ wide × ½″ thick

Flippers (2): 2½″ long × ⅞″ wide × ¼″ thick

Flukes (2): 2¾″ long × 1½″ wide × ½″ thick

Eyes: 3mm

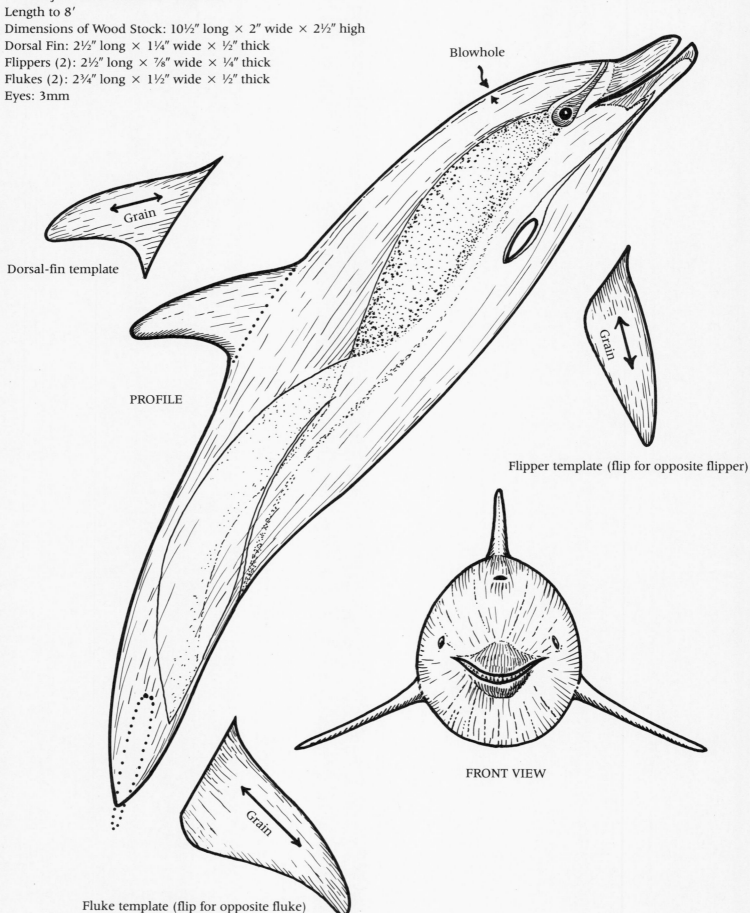

Dorsal-fin template

Grain

Blowhole

PROFILE

Grain

Flipper template (flip for opposite flipper)

FRONT VIEW

Grain

Fluke template (flip for opposite fluke)

Plate 3 *(left)*

Remove staples to see and use full patterns.

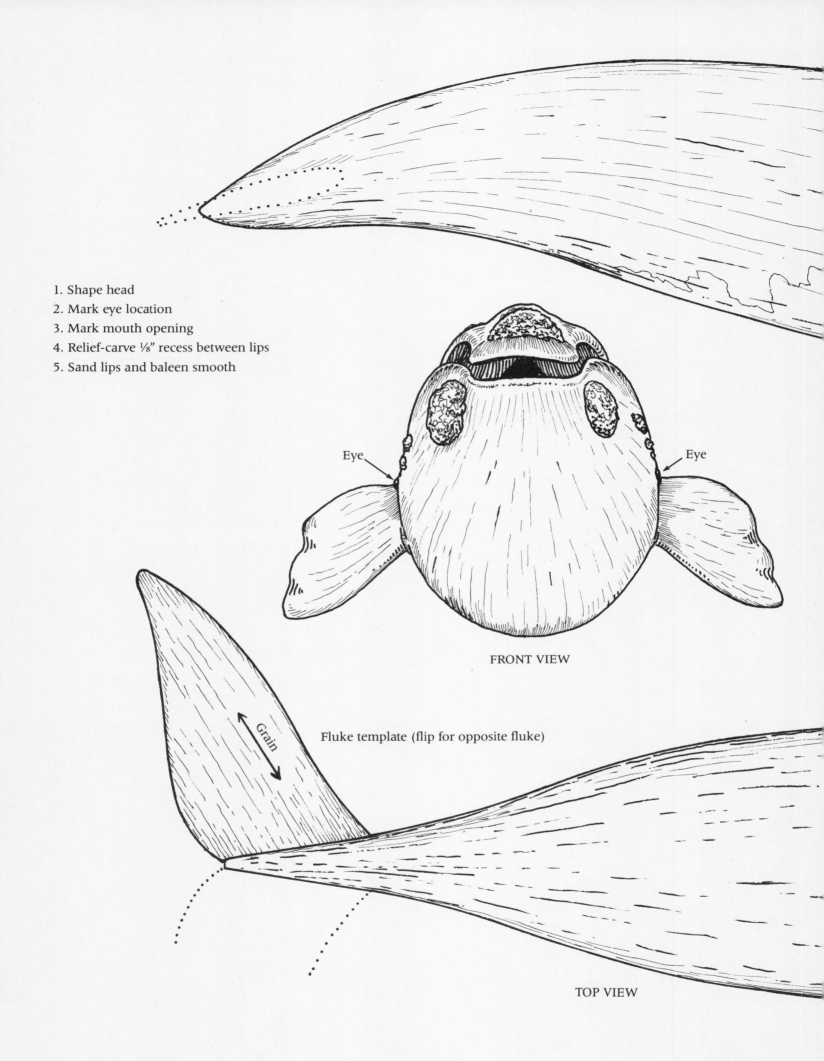

1. Shape head
2. Mark eye location
3. Mark mouth opening
4. Relief-carve ⅛″ recess between lips
5. Sand lips and baleen smooth

Eye

Eye

FRONT VIEW

Grain

Fluke template (flip for opposite fluke)

TOP VIEW

Plate 4 *(left)*

Remove staples to see and use full patterns.

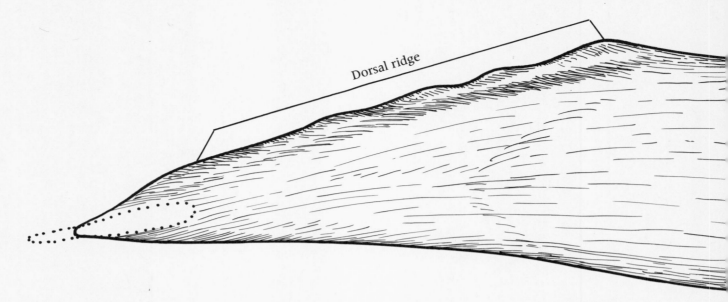

Dorsal ridge

PROFILE

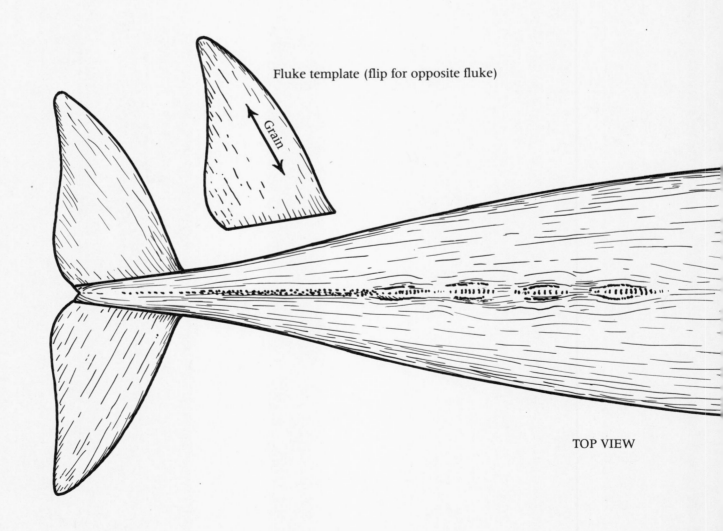

Fluke template (flip for opposite fluke)

Grain

TOP VIEW

Plate 5 *(left)*

Remove staples to see and use full patterns.

Long-finned Pilot Whale.

Highly migratory but found mostly in northerly temperate and Arctic waters, this whale is really a huge dolphin, some individuals weighing as much as three tons. The similar Short-finned Pilot Whale inhabits warmer waters.

Length to 19'
Dimensions of Wood Stock: 12¾" long × 2¾" wide × 3¾" high
Flippers (2): 3" long × 1" wide × ¾" thick
Flukes (2): 3" long × 1½" wide × ¾" thick
Eyes: 3mm

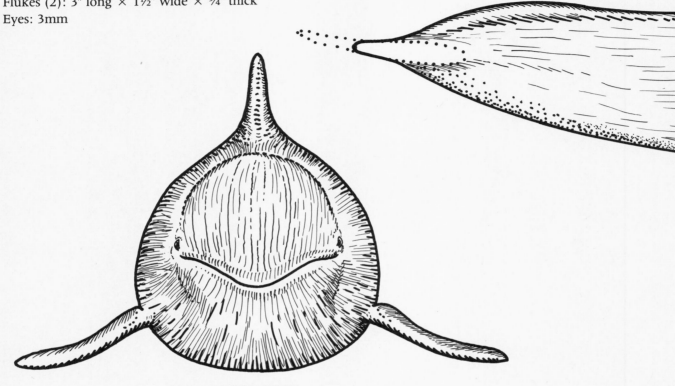

FRONT VIEW

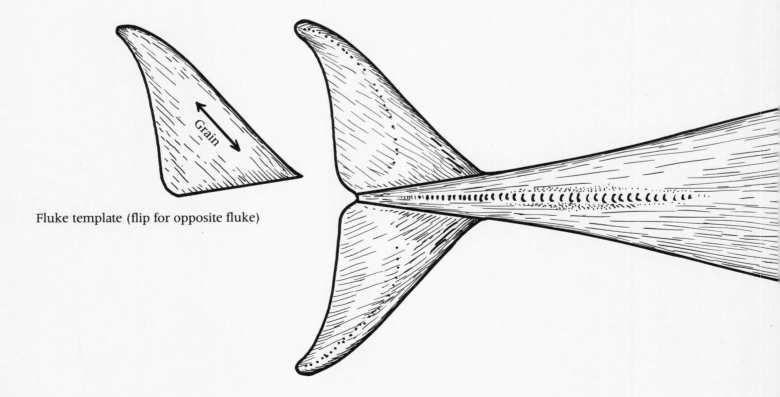

Grain

Fluke template (flip for opposite fluke)

Plate 6 (left)

Remove staples to see and use full patterns.

Cross section of tail stock

Grain

FRONT VIEW

Fluke template (flip for opposite fluke)

Grain

Bottom view of adult Killer Whale

Plate 7 *(left)*

Remove staples to see and use full patterns.

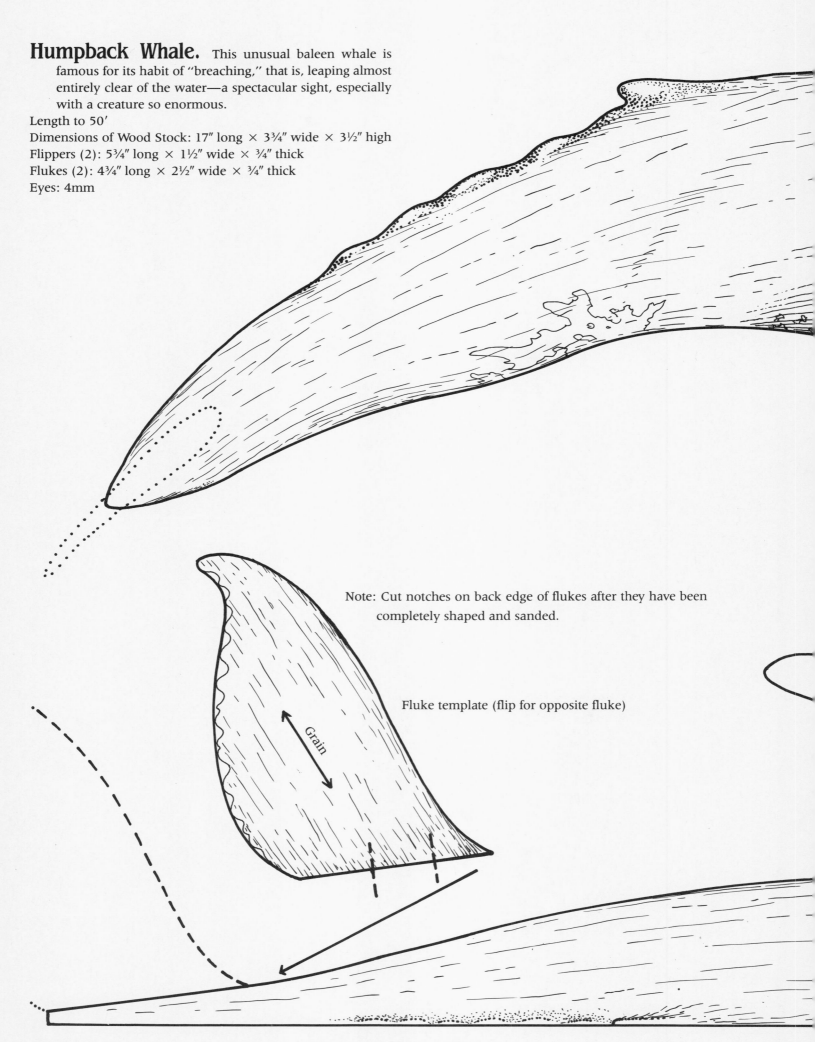

Humpback Whale.
This unusual baleen whale is famous for its habit of "breaching," that is, leaping almost entirely clear of the water—a spectacular sight, especially with a creature so enormous.

Length to 50'

Dimensions of Wood Stock: 17" long × 3¾" wide × 3½" high

Flippers (2): 5¾" long × 1½" wide × ¾" thick

Flukes (2): 4¾" long × 2½" wide × ¾" thick

Eyes: 4mm

Note: Cut notches on back edge of flukes after they have been completely shaped and sanded.

Fluke template (flip for opposite fluke)

Grain

Plate 8 *(left)*

Remove staples to see and use full patterns.

Bottlenose Dolphin. Well known from sightings along both coasts of the United States, as well as many other parts of the world, this playful animal is even better known as an intelligent and versatile performer in aquatic shows.

Length to 12'

Dimensions of Wood Stock: 12½" long × 2½" wide × 2¾" high

Dorsal Fin: 2½" long × 1¾" wide × ½" thick

Flippers (2): 2¾" long × 1" wide × ½" thick

Flukes (2): 2¾" long × 1½" wide × ¾" thick

Eyes: 3mm

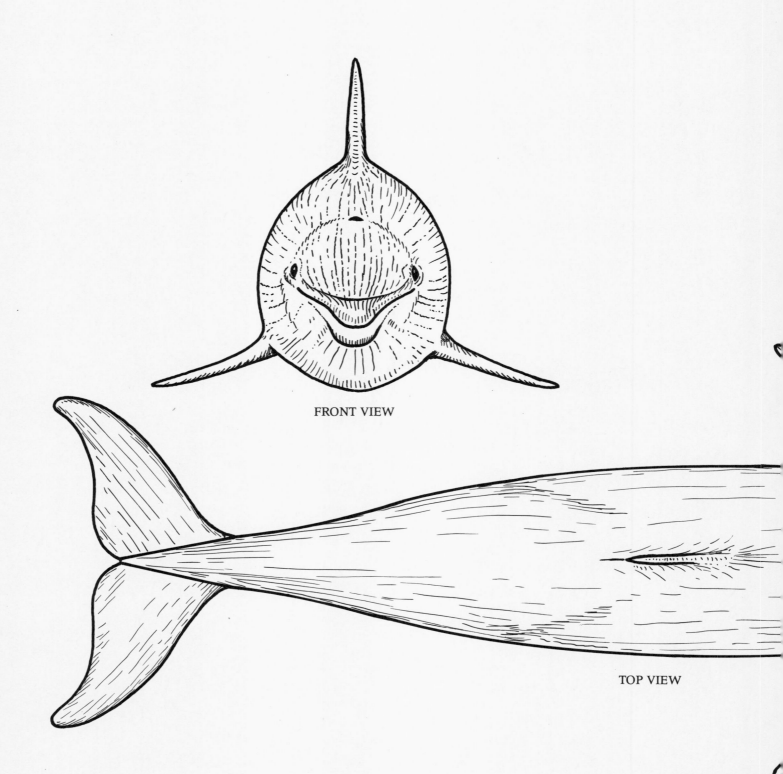

FRONT VIEW

TOP VIEW

Plate 9 *(left)*

Remove staples to see and use full patterns.

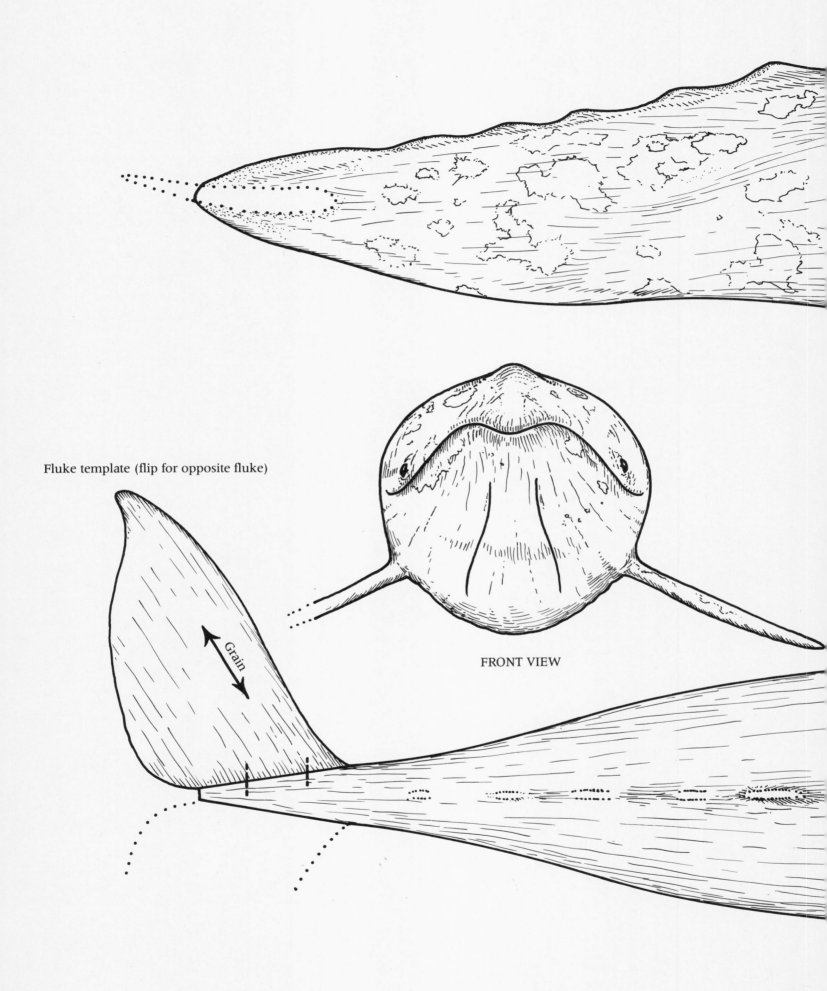

Fluke template (flip for opposite fluke)

Grain

FRONT VIEW

Plate 10 *(left)*

Remove staples to see and use full patterns.

PROFILE

Flipper template (flip for opposite flipper)

Tail sawn and carved with body

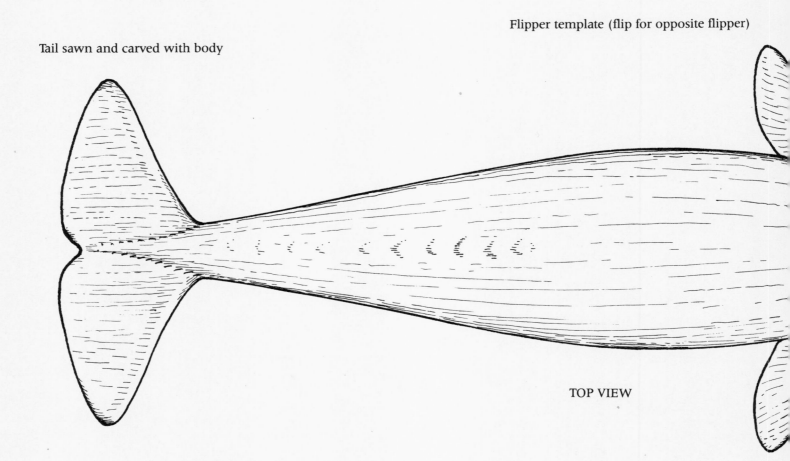

TOP VIEW

Plate 11 *(left)*

Remove staples to see and use full patterns.

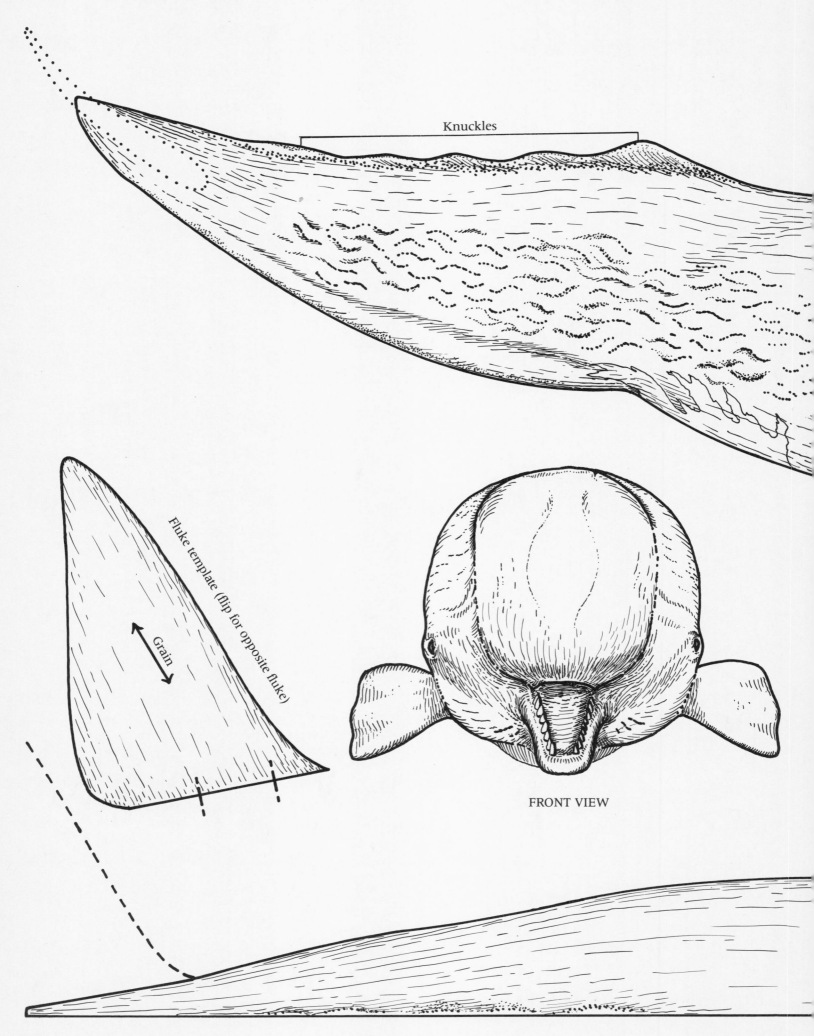

Knuckles

Fluke template (flip for opposite fluke)

Grain

FRONT VIEW

Plate 12 *(left)*

Remove staples to see and use full patterns.

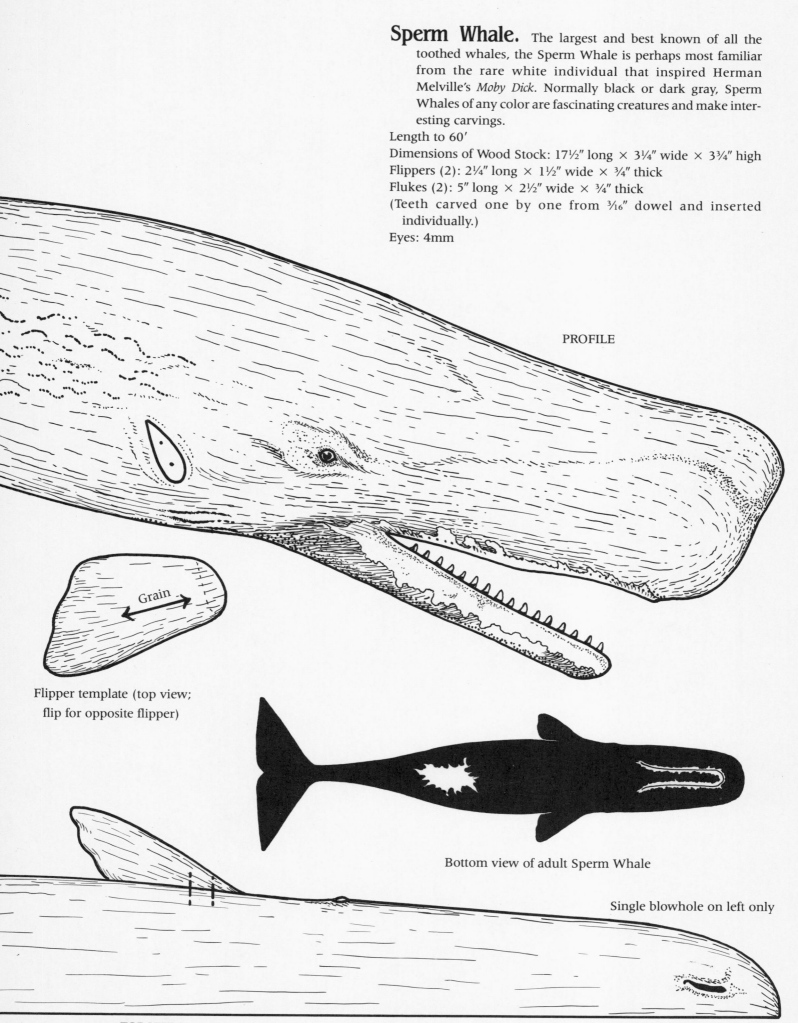

Sperm Whale. The largest and best known of all the toothed whales, the Sperm Whale is perhaps most familiar from the rare white individual that inspired Herman Melville's *Moby Dick*. Normally black or dark gray, Sperm Whales of any color are fascinating creatures and make interesting carvings.

Length to 60′

Dimensions of Wood Stock: 17½″ long × 3¼″ wide × 3¾″ high

Flippers (2): 2¼″ long × 1½″ wide × ¾″ thick

Flukes (2): 5″ long × 2½″ wide × ¾″ thick

(Teeth carved one by one from ³⁄₁₆″ dowel and inserted individually.)

Eyes: 4mm

PROFILE

Grain

Flipper template (top view;
flip for opposite flipper)

Bottom view of adult Sperm Whale

Single blowhole on left only

TOP VIEW

Remove staples to see and use full patterns.

Plate 12 *(right)*

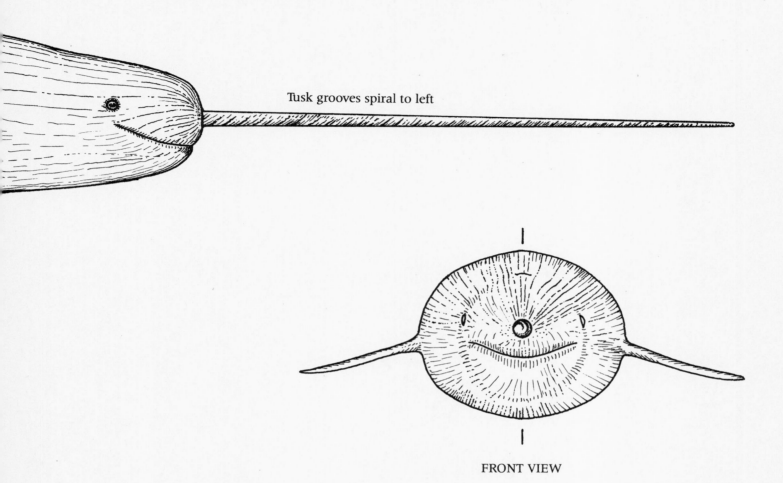

Tusk grooves spiral to left

FRONT VIEW

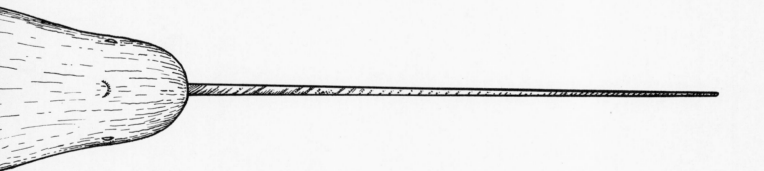

Narwhal. Closely related and similar in appearance to the Beluga (but heavily spotted), the Narwhal also inhabits northern waters, though it is less widely distributed. Narwhals are most unusual for their enormous twisted tusk, which is really a gigantic tooth! In olden days this tusk was often passed off as the horn of the mythical unicorn.

Length to 16′

Dimensions of Wood Stock: 10½″ long × 4″ wide × 2¼″ high

Flippers (2): 1½″ long × ¾″ wide × ¼″ thick

(Flukes sawn and carved with body.)

Tusk: ³⁄₁₆″ dowel, 6½″ long

Eyes: 3mm

PROFILE

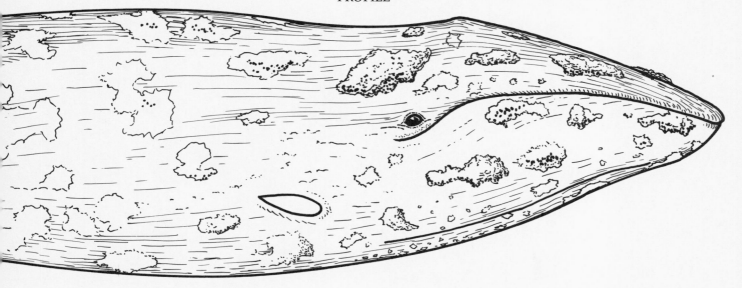

Gray Whale. This Pacific Coast baleen whale is not closely related to any other whale. Highly migratory, it travels farther than any other mammal on earth, some ten thousand miles a year.

Length to 45′
Dimensions of Wood Stock: 15″ long × 3″ wide × 3¼″ high
Flippers (2): 2¾″ long × 1¼″ wide × ¾″ thick
Flukes (2): 4″ long × 2¼″ wide × ¾″ thick
Eyes: 4mm

Flipper template (top view; flip for opposite flipper)

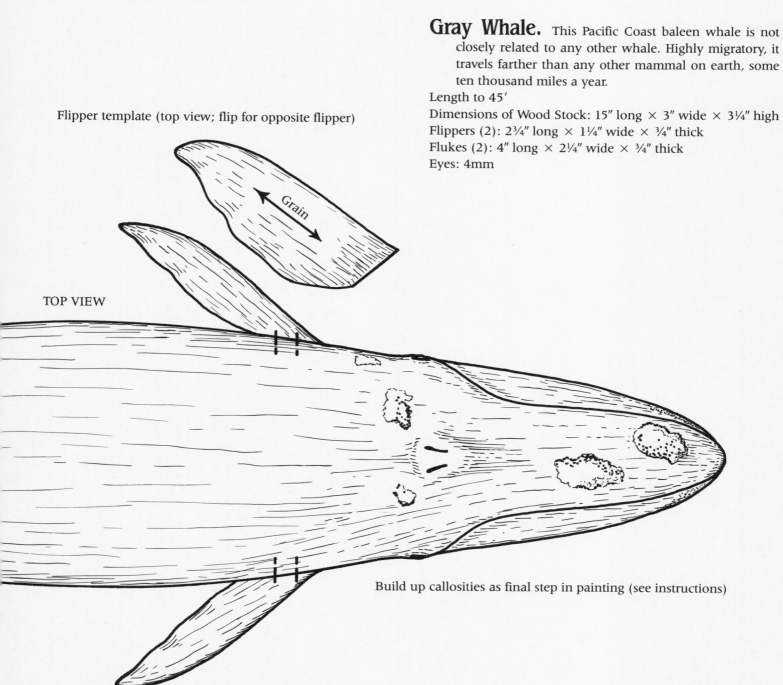

Grain

TOP VIEW

Build up callosities as final step in painting (see instructions)

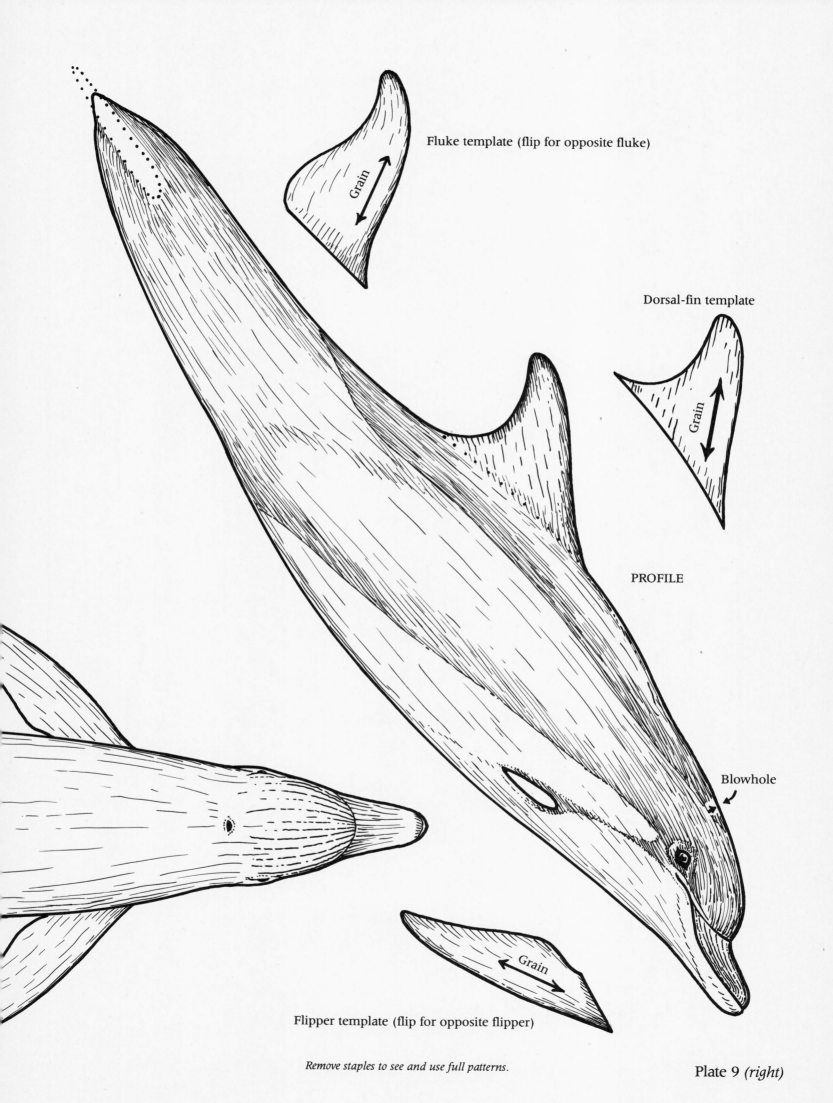

Fluke template (flip for opposite fluke)

Grain

Dorsal-fin template

Grain

PROFILE

Blowhole

Grain

Flipper template (flip for opposite flipper)

Remove staples to see and use full patterns.

Plate 9 *(right)*

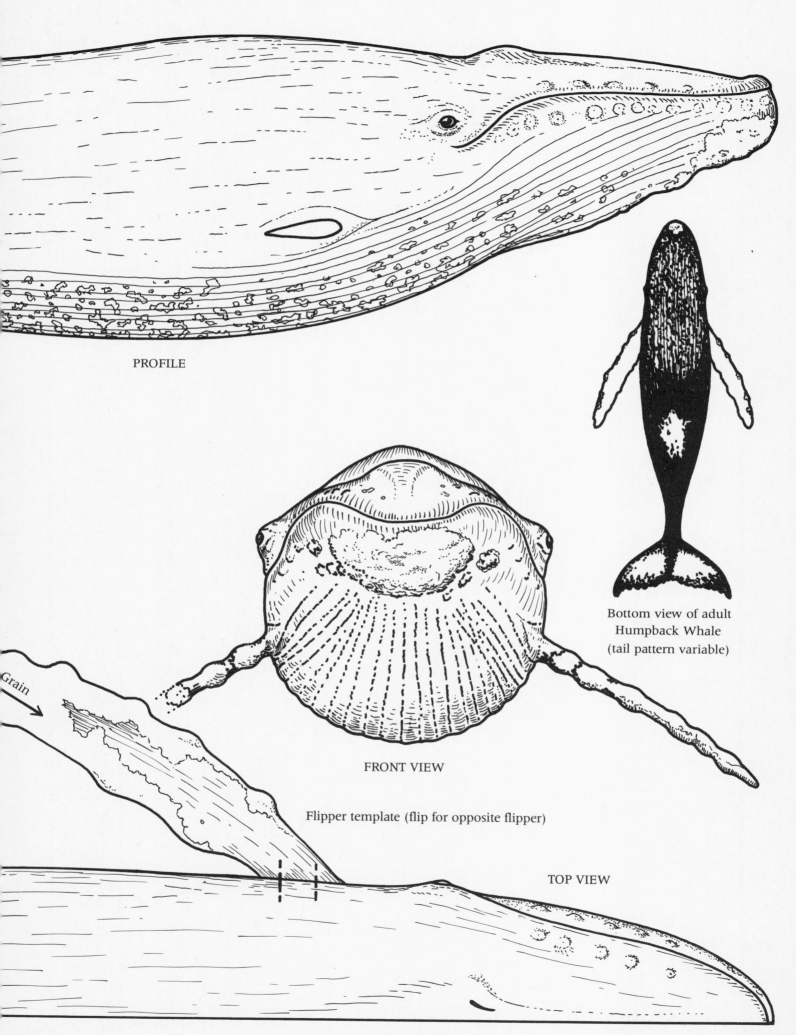

PROFILE

Grain

FRONT VIEW

Flipper template (flip for opposite flipper)

Bottom view of adult
Humpback Whale
(tail pattern variable)

TOP VIEW

Remove staples to see and use full patterns.

Plate 8 *(right)*

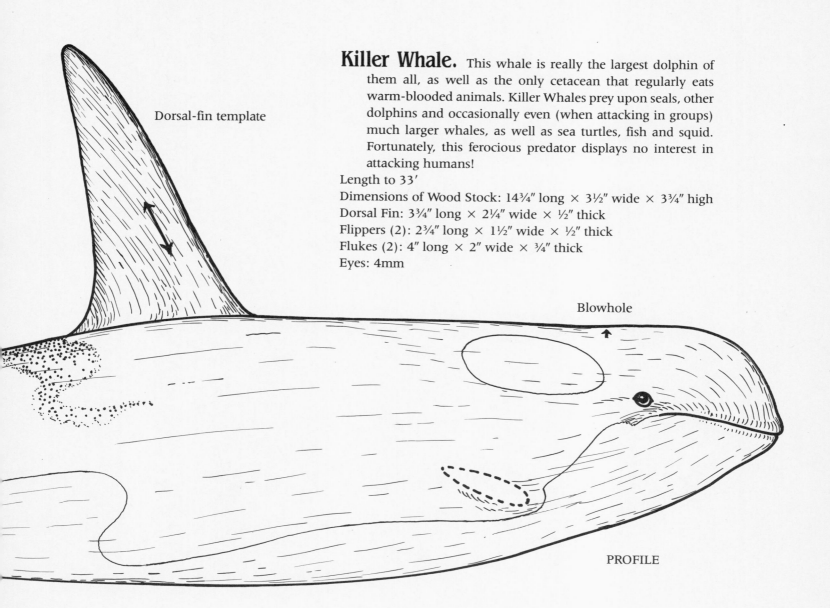

Dorsal-fin template

Killer Whale. This whale is really the largest dolphin of them all, as well as the only cetacean that regularly eats warm-blooded animals. Killer Whales prey upon seals, other dolphins and occasionally even (when attacking in groups) much larger whales, as well as sea turtles, fish and squid. Fortunately, this ferocious predator displays no interest in attacking humans!

Length to 33'
Dimensions of Wood Stock: 14¾" long × 3½" wide × 3¾" high
Dorsal Fin: 3¾" long × 2¼" wide × ½" thick
Flippers (2): 2¾" long × 1½" wide × ½" thick
Flukes (2): 4" long × 2" wide × ¾" thick
Eyes: 4mm

Blowhole

PROFILE

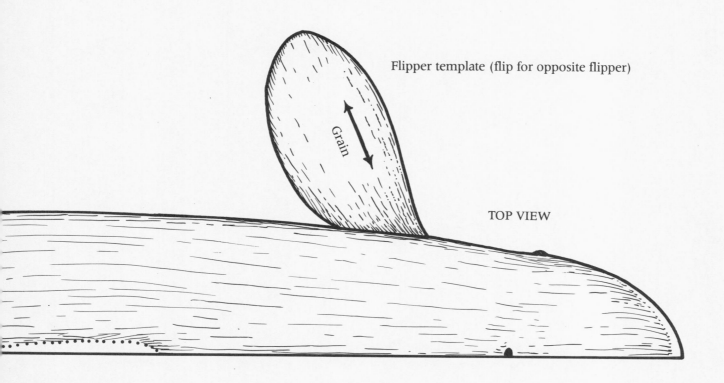

Flipper template (flip for opposite flipper)

Grain

TOP VIEW

Remove staples to see and use full patterns.

Plate 7 *(right)*

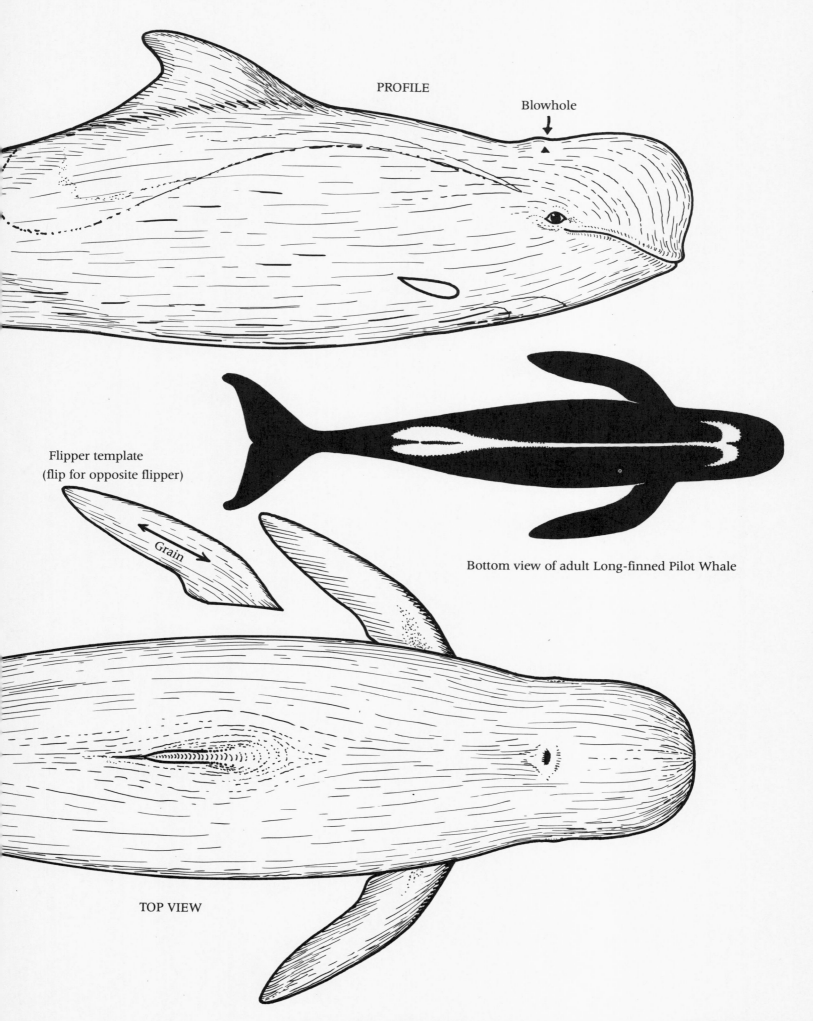

PROFILE

Blowhole

Flipper template
(flip for opposite flipper)

Grain

Bottom view of adult Long-finned Pilot Whale

TOP VIEW

Remove staples to see and use full patterns.

Plate 6 *(right)*

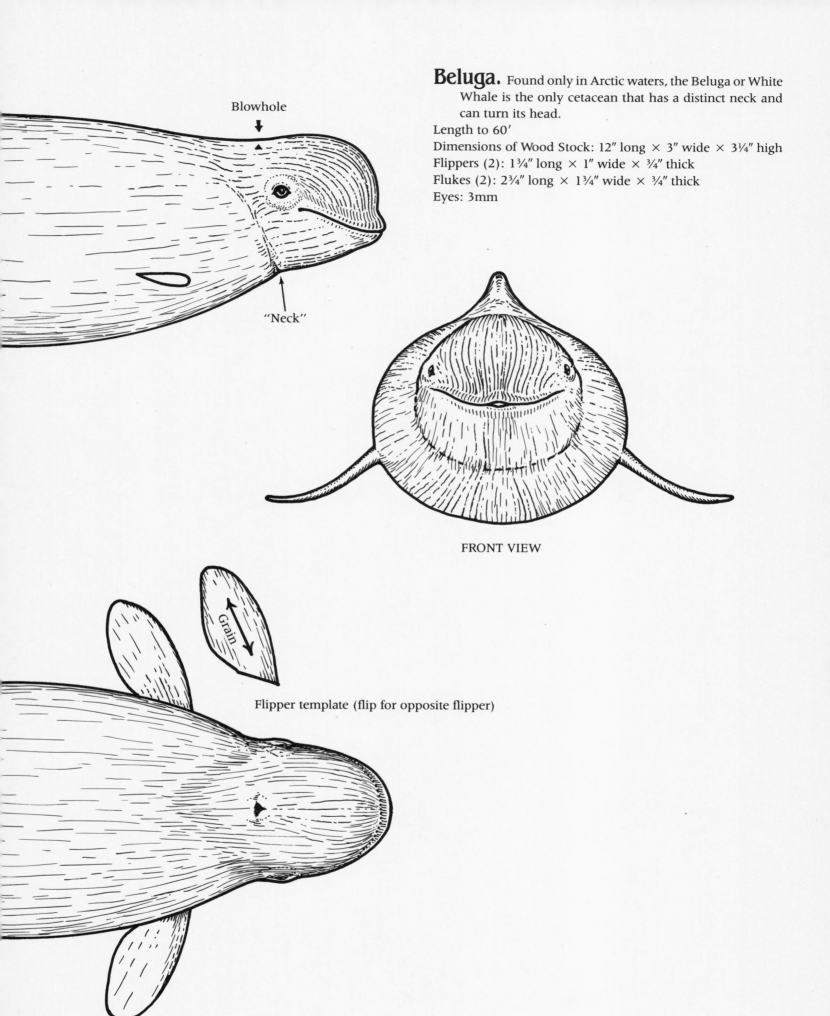

Blowhole

"Neck"

Beluga. Found only in Arctic waters, the Beluga or White Whale is the only cetacean that has a distinct neck and can turn its head.

Length to 60'

Dimensions of Wood Stock: 12" long × 3" wide × 3¼" high

Flippers (2): 1¾" long × 1" wide × ¾" thick

Flukes (2): 2¾" long × 1¾" wide × ¾" thick

Eyes: 3mm

FRONT VIEW

Grain

Flipper template (flip for opposite flipper)

Remove staples to see and use full patterns.

Plate 5 *(right)*

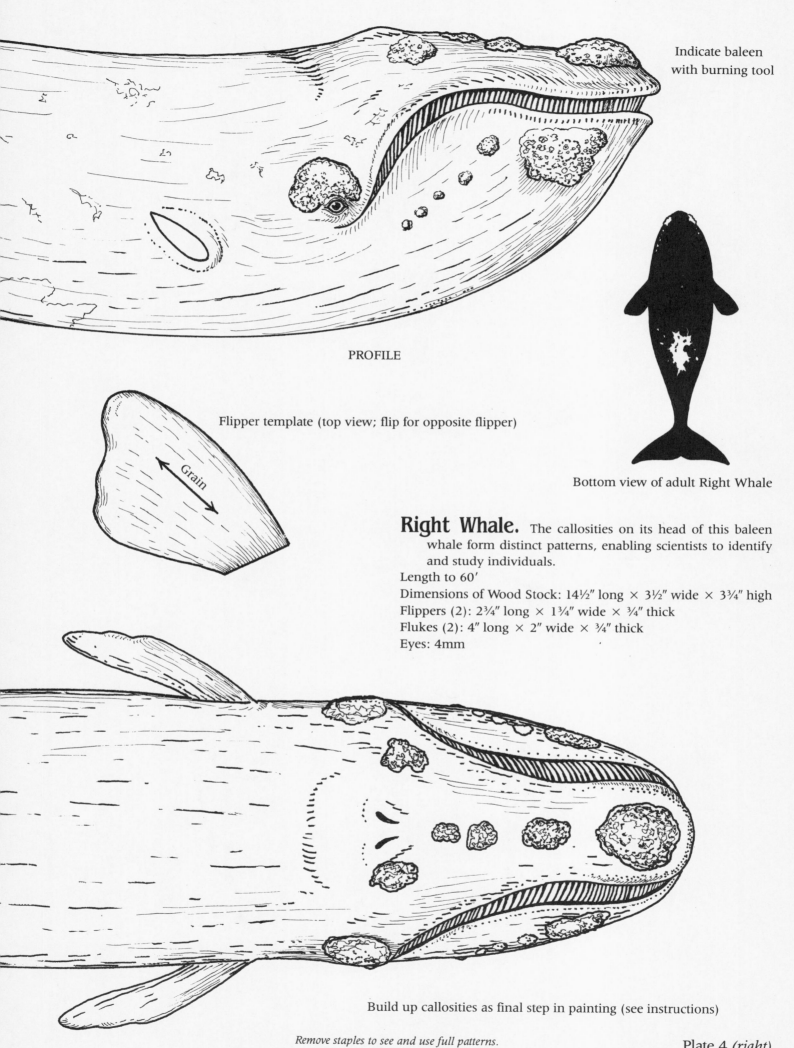

Indicate baleen with burning tool

PROFILE

Flipper template (top view; flip for opposite flipper)

Grain

Bottom view of adult Right Whale

Right Whale. The callosities on its head of this baleen whale form distinct patterns, enabling scientists to identify and study individuals.
Length to 60′
Dimensions of Wood Stock: 14½″ long × 3½″ wide × 3¾″ high
Flippers (2): 2¾″ long × 1¾″ wide × ¾″ thick
Flukes (2): 4″ long × 2″ wide × ¾″ thick
Eyes: 4mm

Build up callosities as final step in painting (see instructions)

Remove staples to see and use full patterns.

Plate 4 *(right)*

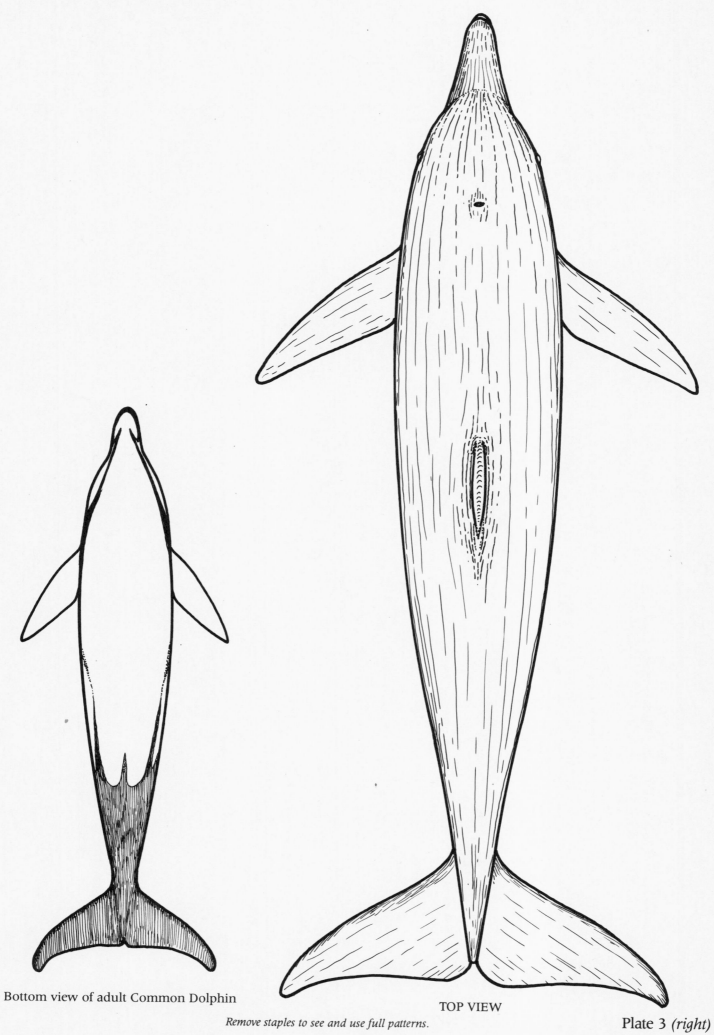

Bottom view of adult Common Dolphin

TOP VIEW

Remove staples to see and use full patterns.

Plate 3 *(right)*

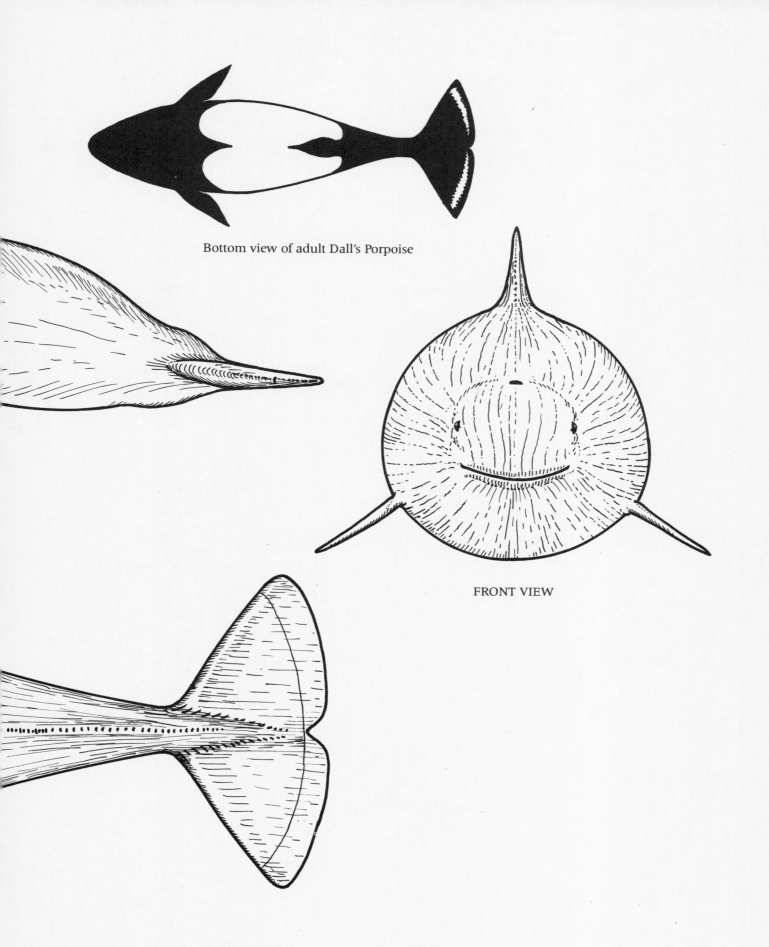

Bottom view of adult Dall's Porpoise

FRONT VIEW

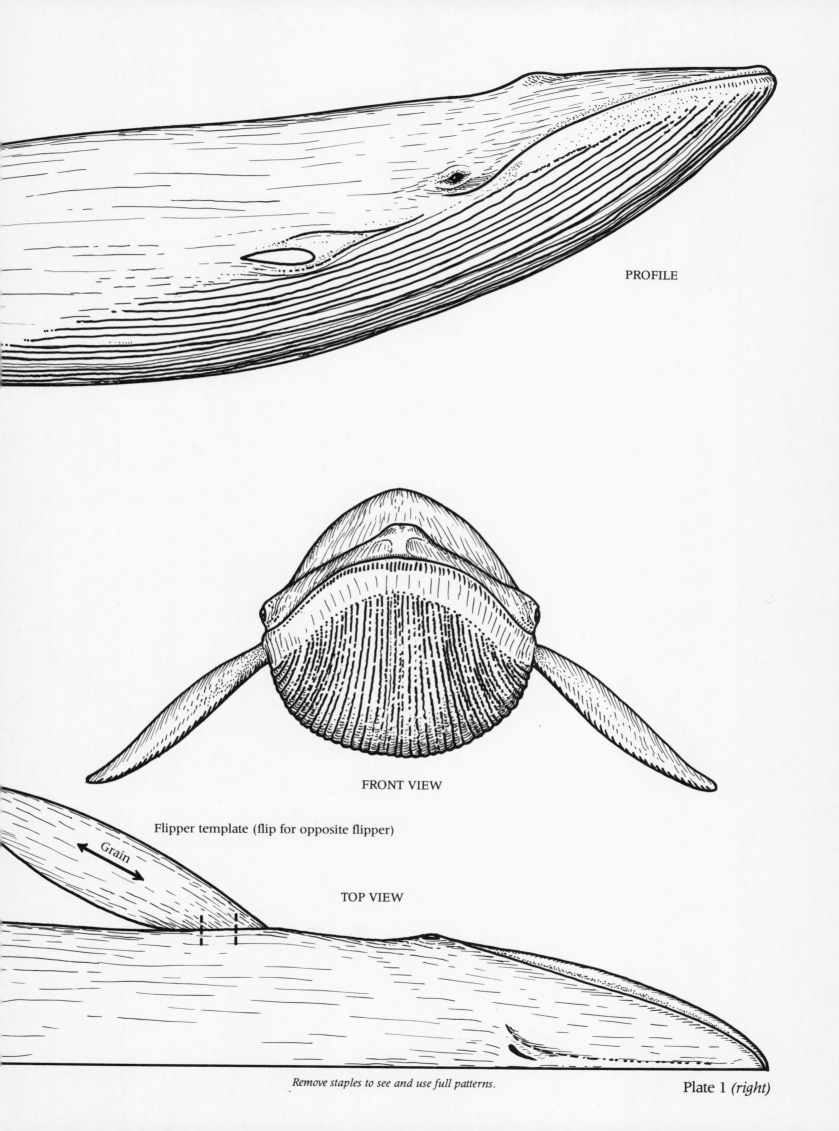

PROFILE

FRONT VIEW

Flipper template (flip for opposite flipper)

Grain

TOP VIEW

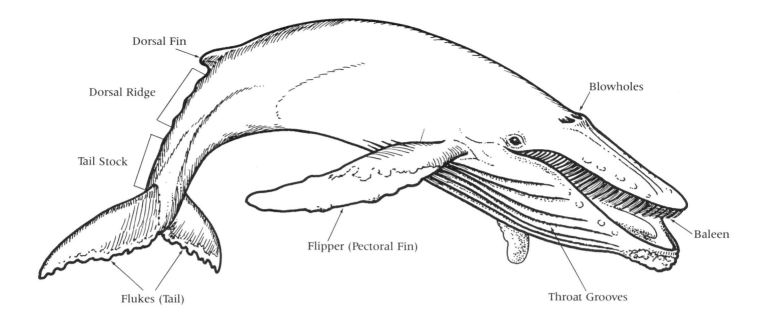

The Parts of a Whale (Humpback Whale)

cially the Beluga. Whalers called this anatomical feature the "knuckles" on whales and that is a good comparison.

Other species have a dorsal fin *and* several knuckles behind it. A good example of this kind of whale is the Humpback. Your first carving task will be to carve "downhill" (Fig. 3) from the highest point of the profile (usually a dorsal or ridge). At this stage we are roughing out the block and removing most of the wood from the corners of the blank and at the same time considering those important anatomical features unique (however subtle) to each species.

As you remove the wood, try to maintain an orderly progression taking care not to remove more than is necessary from each corner. As you carve keep references handy to guide you. I have already explained how important a proper flush surface is for the tail flukes. On those species that require an add-on dorsal fin (Killer Whale, Common Dolphin and Bottlenose Dolphin), you will need to be careful not to alter your

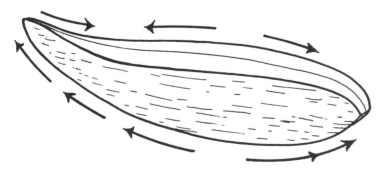

Fig. 3. Direction of Carving

cut-out blank at the point where this fin will be placed (see Fig. 2). That is so that you can mate the dorsal fin to the body since the base of the fin pattern follows the exact curve of the body.

For now it is enough that your carving reflect the shape shown in the reference drawings on the Plates.

The area where the flippers go on the body need not be considered as you give the body its general shape. As you carve down the head it will help to pencil in the location of the eyes and mouth for reference.

As you gradually take the carving down to the desired proportions, keep checking what you have done against the patterns and the photographic references. A small gouge is often useful for defining the areas around the "knuckles." I also use a small spokeshave to give the rounded, sleek contours needed for the body and tail stock.

It is a good idea to finish the body contours as much as possible including the head, being careful to pay attention to mouth parts as required. The Beluga, the Dall's Porpoise, the Common and Bottlenose Dolphins and the Long-finned Pilot Whale require careful shaping of their mouth parts.

I have presented the Right Whale carving with his mouth open enough to show the baleen plates. The lips are first outlined and defined with relief carving. Wood is removed between the lips so that there is an even recess all the way around. After sanding the face of the baleen smooth and finish-sanding the lips, the baleen lines are burned in with a burning tool.

Rorqual whales all have furrows or folds of skin that extend below the jaw along the throat to beyond their flippers. The purpose of these grooves is to allow tremendous expansion of the throat so that water laden with krill or other tiny creatures can be rapidly filtered. Once you have shaped and sanded this area on the two rorquals in this book—the Humpback Whale (which, somewhat confusingly, is often classified outside of the rorquals in a one-species group of its own) and the Blue Whale—cut in the grooves with a V-parting tool or very small gouge. Repeat the finish-sanding *in* the grooves when carving is complete.

Once you are satisfied that you have carved your subject as close to the finished contours as you can, mark the areas where any dorsal, pectoral or tail fins are to be attached to the carving.

Finish-sand the entire carving, being careful not to alter the areas where the fins will be "mated" to the carving.

Carve the blowhole (or blowholes—the patterns show which species have two). Now drill the eye sockets and insert the proper-size glass eyes. Seal around the edges of the eye holes with wood filler if necessary.

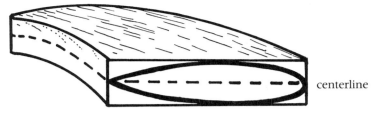

Fig. 5. Fluke

Fig. 6. Fin Showing Teardrop Shape

CARVING FLIPPERS, FLUKES AND DORSAL FINS

Cut out each template as required. I have provided a single template for each tail fluke, dorsal fin and flipper, as you will require just one template for both tail flukes. This enables you to achieve symmetry: just trace the pattern, then flip it over and trace the symmetrical pattern for the other fluke.

Saw out the fin, fluke or flipper, paying careful attention to grain direction as indicated on the template.

I have given ample wood measurements to ensure plenty of carving space around the template. If you possess a jigsaw, you can sandwich the sawn-out shape between two scrap pieces (to keep your fingers clear of the blade) and cut a *front view* curve for each flipper or the dorsal fin. The tail flukes can be done the same way (see Fig. 4). Once these have been sawn out, draw a centerline completely around the fin and pencil in the proper elongated teardrop shape on the base of each (Fig. 5). Carry this shape through the entire fin or fluke (Fig. 6). Carefully carve each fin as required, referring to the patterns. Sand smooth to finish.

ATTACHING FLUKES, FLIPPERS AND DORSAL FINS

Once the pieces have been carefully shaped and sanded, you must test-fit them to their proper locations on the carving. The flippers require an angular slice of wood to be cut from their base so that they lie properly slanted in relation to the body. It will probably require several tries at fitting, cutting and fitting again before success. To ensure a perfect fit, especially of flippers and dorsal fins, I use self-stick sandpaper. A piece of this will adhere to the body in the desired location. Then I simply hold the fin at the desired angle and carefully rub back and forth. This finish-sands the fin base to the exact contour of that location. I then take one or (if the fin is a larger one) two brass hobby pins and push these into the base of the fin. After the pins are halfway into the fin, I cut off the pin heads with wire cutters. Then, adding yellow carpenter's glue to the surface and, keeping the correct angle, I push the fin onto the body. With practice this procedure becomes a simple operation (see Fig. 7). Allow all fins done this way to dry for at least four hours. Then fill in any gaps with glue, and allow to dry again until the glue has thoroughly hardened. (Note: On

Fig. 4. Front View of Flukes

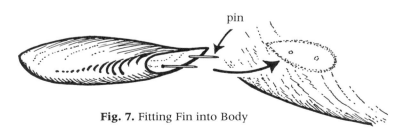

Fig. 7. Fitting Fin into Body

some plates you will see pins indicated by dashed lines; these lines do not appear on some plates, however, even when pins must be used. This is so as not to interfere with smooth cutting when using the patterns. Wherever a flipper or fluke is carved separately, it must be attached with pins and glue.)

When dry, sand the joints with #220 or finer sandpaper. If necessary, smooth the joint with wood filler and sand when dry. Check the entire carving for a smooth accurate finish-sanding. Remove all dust that has accumulated from the sanding, being careful not to break the fins!

SEALING AND FINISHING YOUR CARVING

There are several sealers available to protect the carving from moisture and dirt. A common method of sealing a woodcarving is to coat it with shellac cut fifty percent with alcohol. Water-based sanding sealers are also now available. These are safe and have little odor.

I recommend using two coats of sealer. Sand between coats.

As for a paint primer, I always use exterior latex primer on my carvings. Since most of these creatures are black or shades of gray, it is a good idea to use a dark primer. That way if your carving is scratched, the dark primer that is exposed will not be as obvious as a lighter one would be. Again, it is usually necessary to apply two coats. Sand between coats.

Once you have sealed and primed your carving, you are ready to paint it. All cetaceans have a wet, sleek look, making gloss or semigloss paints appropriate. Two coats of body color are usually sufficient.

The range of colors on whales and dolphins is not extensive, yet even an all-black whale will usually have scars, callosities (bony skin growths that are usually creamy white) and a subtle mottling caused by an underlying secondary color. For those species with a distinctive color pattern I have indicated that pattern as far as possible on the cutting patterns. The common dolphin is an extreme case, with a unique, extremely subtle pattern that will simply make you crazy the first time you try to paint it on a carving! Naturally, I don't recommend that you make this your first project unless you already have some experience in painting woodcarvings. (In nature, these dolphins show considerable variation in their coloration; I have indicated the basic scheme.)

If you are carving the species that have callosities, you can duplicate these pale bony growths by using modeling paste mixed with an off-white paint. It may be necessary to build up several coats to get the right look.

When you are satisfied that the carving is complete,

you may want to apply a clear gloss finish or simply use paste wax on your carving to protect it.

DISPLAYING YOUR CARVING

You have several options for displaying your work. You can mount it on a formal wooden base, mount it less formally on a piece of driftwood, or perhaps suspend your carving by hanging it on an overhead hook by a thin monofilament line.

I hope you have as much fun carving these interesting animals as I did.

A NOTE ON SUPPLIERS

You may be able to buy such items as glass eyes where you obtain your woodcarving and painting tools and materials. Check your local classified telephone directory. The following mail-order suppliers carry stocks of glass eyes and cast feet. It is a good idea to write or telephone for information before ordering.

Wood Carvers Supply, Inc.
P.O. Box 7500
Englewood, FL 34295
Telephone (Information): (941) 698-0123
Telephone (Orders): (800) 284-6229

Craftwoods
2101 Greenspring Drive
P.O. Box 527
Timonium, MD 21094
Telephone (Catalogs and Customer Service):
 (410) 561-9470
Telephone (Sales): (800) 468-7070

RECOMMENDED REFERENCE BOOKS

Carwardine, Mark. Illus. by Martin Camm. *Whales, Dolphins, and Porpoises: The Visual Guide to All the World's Cetaceans.* Eyewitness Handbooks, published by Dorling Kindersley Publishing, Inc., New York, 1995. Extensive color illustrations.

Leatherwood, Stephen, Randall R. Reeves, William F. Perrin and William E. Evans. *Whales, Dolphins, and Porpoises of the Eastern North Pacific and Adjacent Arctic Waters: A Guide to Their Identification.* Dover Publications, Inc., New York, 1988 (originally published 1982). (ISBN: 0-486-25651-0.) Includes extensive black-and-white photos of cetaceans.